W9-CHG-192

My Marriage A to z

A Big-City Romance

My Marriage A to Z

A Big-City Romance

by Elinor Nauen

My Marriage A to Z : A Big City Romance

Printed in the United States.

First Edition
10 9 8 7 6 5 4 3 2 1

Library of Congress Cataloging-in-Publication Data

Nauen, Elinor.

My marriage A to Z : a big city romance / by Elinor Nauen ;
Illustrations by Sophy Naess. — 1st ed.
p. cm.

ISBN 978-1-935955-04-7 (alk. paper)
1. Marriage—Poetry. I. Title.
PS3564.A8736M9 2012
811'.54—dc22

2011011456

Book and cover design by Mona Pennypacker.
All the girls are coming back home!

for Johnny, as everything is always for Johnny,
and also: to newlyweds Will and Sarafina

Assassin. We were in the West Village, on 4th and Mercer, across from the Bottom Line. A Sunday morning, just swinging along, thinking about breakfast and the book tables by Washington Square Park. A little old man with a neat white beard and black beret passed us. I barely noticed him until Johnny said, "Did you see that guy? He was a famous mob hit man when I was a kid."

"Wow!" I said. "But I didn't get a good look. Can we walk around him?"

"Absolutely not," Johnny said.

Later, when I told my mother, she said, "I would trust Johnny Stanton when it comes to assassin etiquette."

My sister Varda, who refers to Johnny as The Most Handsome Stanton in Manhattan, said, "I'd trust him too. After all, wasn't he called the 18-year-old knife fighter in that poem of Ted Berrigan's?"

After I'd told people for years about my husband recognizing an actual murderer, Johnny finally told me that he'd made up the story on the spot. When I believed it so excitedly and unquestioningly, he didn't have the heart to tell me the truth.

Anniversaries. He once told me, "Go in the other room I brought you something happy anniversary." It was a humidifier, not even wrapped, and I thought I would divorce him. ... He's learned. These days he buys me beautiful gifts, things he knows will please me, such as necklaces he designs himself. By now, though, I would rather have a new humidifier.

Arguing Tone of Voice. With one exception, the only thing I've learned from anyone else's marriage is: I don't want to be like that. The exception: Some counsel we got early on sustains our own 26-year relationship. It's called Not Arguing Tone of Voice. It means we refrain from the malicious pleasure of declaring "I don't like the way you said that," and instead are required to stick with the matter at hand. (See *Fines*.) Not unrelatedly, we are ridiculously polite. Please, thank you, excuse me, bless you, with the occasional prompts of "What's the magic word?"

Beginning, in the. One day in 1983, I told my friend I was unable to read anything but the tabloids. "Are you in love?" she said.

Bed. One time Johnny and I were comp'ed at a very fancy hotel in Washington, D.C. Our room had the most enormous bed I've ever seen, a siamese king. In the morning Johnny told me he hadn't slept well. "I kept reaching for you in the night," he said, "and I couldn't find you." It's one of those moments when you know you are inextricably linked. At home we have a double mattress, which we share with loads of books, pillows and a cat. We never aren't touching. Hand to hand, skin to skin.

Bets. In practically our first-ever conversation, I won $20 betting he was wrong about the name of the old TV show being *My Mother-in-Law the Car*. I mocked his ear: Hollywood would never go with such a clunky title! It's *My Mother the Car*! He handed over that $20 without blinking, and I gloated. Was he setting me up? He has won pretty much every bet since then. I currently owe him $280,000 for claiming that Florence is (isn't?) in Tuscany.

Bass. I do like Johnny's occasional protective moments. Today he warned me not to ride my bicycle. The streets are too slippery, he said. He was very insistent, and I finally said I would walk, then—what did he expect?—rode off on my bike.

Bass, the. Johnny saw Bruce Springsteen on 72nd Street. "Congratulations, man!" Johnny hollered.

"Thanks! What for?"

Johnny talks before he thinks. "For your ... children!" he said.

"Thanks, man!"

Boyfriends. I never had so many boyfriends until I got married. They love me for being happy elsewhere.

Camping.   Johnny said he knew his first marriage was over when she came home with a sleeping bag and a tent. My personal belief is that my ancestors spent two million years crawling out of the primordial ooze, and the least I can do is stay out of it. We did used to go camping every year with a bunch of friends to Lake Sebago, just north of the city, but we stayed in cabins and the principal activity was guarding (and drinking) the wine.

Chicken Soup.   Once when I had a cold, I asked Johnny to get me chicken soup from the Kiev, a Ukrainian diner five blocks away. *Mmmm, chicken soup, thick with veggies and noodles. The most comforting food in the world.* He was back suspiciously fast. Turned out he'd gone to the deli downstairs and brought back a can of fat-free chicken broth. Then he pouted that I didn't appreciate him and wouldn't go back out for the real thing. And I cried for the lack of soup and sympathy. Thank goodness for my sister, and my best friend and the city of New York, or I would have no emotional life at all.

City Hall. We'd known each other 12 years and had been going out for eight when we made our way to the Municipal Building in lower Manhattan on December 23, 1991. He was wearing the bowtie from his daughter's bunny suit, a striped t-shirt and had shaggy hair. I wore a borrowed black-suede dress and motorcycle boots. We picked City Hall because I didn't want a wedding, but the wedding followed us there. Everyone I ran into that week asked what was I doing for the holidays. Getting married, I told them, and one after another they said, "I'm not doing anything Monday." You must come, I responded politely, and they did, some 20 people: Johnny's 10-year-old daughter; my brother; a handful of friends who happened to be in town; the poet Eileen Myles, my best man, as I had been hers; even my dentist, Ruth, and her two kids. And Ruth brought her camera so I ended up with a wedding album. When Dan ("I'll be marrying you today") asked the crucial "do you take this woman," Johnny replied with a resounding YES. When he asked me, I thought, "Wow, that's a pretty big question. I'm not sure I can answer till I think this through a little. I mean, if I say yes, I'll be married. That's scary but the thought of losing him is scarier, isn't it? I mean—" Johnny's throat-clearing jumped me off the cliff. Later, he said he was jealous of my comic timing. He's never believed I was finally deliberating on what the heck I was doing.

Couple, our. It used to be Doug and Alice, till they moved to Paris. Now it's Kevin and Steve. There are many requirements. Each pair has to get along: that makes six combinations that all have to work. It can't be two friends dragging their spouses to dinner.

Diamonds are a girl's best friend. One kind or another. Funny that I love baseball so much and married one of the few guys who don't.

Divorce. For us the better came after the worse. While we were still rubbing off each other's sharp edges in our first few years together, we indulged in frequent trashy breakups.

Death. Our friend Ted dying made us fall into each other's arms. People dying make us value each other in the front of our hearts, always and right now.

"*Ever-lovin'*" and "*co-vivant*." What he called me on documents before we wed. Nicer than partner, girlfriend or POSSLQ (See POSSLQ). Nicer than wife, for that matter.

Falling in love. I dreamed about him before
I knew him, before I ever came to New York. I dreamed
of hands like a Dürer engraving, every line and shadow
and shred in moonshine clarity. I thought they were Peter's
hands, and remembered better from the dream than from his
caresses. They weren't my father's either. And then I woke up
with Johnny's dreamy dream hands on me and I knew.

First Date. I'm not sure we had a first
date. I met him at a poets' theater festival in 1979.
Then a bunch of us went to Connecticut to see a
girl we knew in a play. Johnny drove us in his work
truck and I insisted on sitting up front, because I like
watching the highway go by. It give him the wrong
idea. The first time we went somewhere together,
just the two of us, he almost killed us racing home,
thinking he was about to get in my pants. I thought
he was a great driver, but when he ran the light on
42nd and First, I knew it was sex not automotive
prowess that powered him.

Fines. When Johnny used to get mad, way back when, I would bust out crying: It was the only thing that would make him stop yelling at me. He finally caught on: "You're doing that on purpose!" This led to our most stabilizing practice, a system (See *Systems*) of $5 fines intended to herd us into considerate behavior. I had to pay for manipulative crying, he for standing me up without notice when he decides to hit a museum (and for dangling bugs he killed with his bare hands in my face), and both of us for arguing tone of voice. (See *Arguing Tone of Voice*.)

Gettysburg. I experienced the entire Civil War via bus tour, museum, film, cyclorama and copious inspection of every single marker on that extensive battlefield. It's important to be a good sport. Once.

Hate. Until you marry, you can't know what it's like to truly hate.

Hair. If I ask him, "Do you notice anything different about me?" he knows that the only answer, said enthusiastically, has to be: "You did something to your hair! It looks great!" All married men are supposed to know this.

Happy Birthday. Johnny used to be a moving man: "a strong back and a weak mind," he'd say. But one thing he never could carry is a tune. That doesn't stop him from performing a loopy, lounge-lizardy version of the birthday song for everyone he knows. Our nieces and nephews don't feel it's really their day until he's called and serenaded them.

Harvey. For some reason, when I mention my husband, many people automatically assume I am making him up. My friend Dot calls him my Rent-a-Husband. One guy explained that I was a "free spirit"—apparently the opposite of a wife. My Uncle Earl always called Johnny "Harvey," after the invisible rabbit. My sister Varda got married six months after we did and generously suggested a little party for us during her weekend. Unfortunately, Johnny's mother died the day before the wedding, so we had to have the party without him. Earl believed till the day he died that I was single.

Hometown, My. "You should come see where I grew up in South Dakota," I said.

"I don't need to," he said. "I know you now."

Hotels. He's not much for vacations, partly because he's not much for staying in hotels. "What's the thrill of sleeping on someone else's sheets?"

I extol the pleasures of hotel life: Magic Fingers! Room service! Ice!

"You're paying a hundred dollars for ... ice? It's just money down the drain."

"Everything's money down the drain," I counter. "Why go out to eat? Why not just buy a package of turkey franks and roast them on a fork over the stove?"

"Good idea. Except we turned off the gas ten years ago."

Of course we did! We live in Manhattan, the Isle of Assisted Living. We don't cook, we order in. The superintendant shovels, and nice men give you a ride anywhere you want to go when you wave your arm in the air. For a few bucks, people will wash, dry and fold your laundry, paint your nails, and stand on line for you at the passport office.

Inertia. Why didn't we ever split up? Many times, it merely seemed easier to stay than to figure out how to divvy up the books.

And then we broke on through to the other side... like playing a video game where you suddenly hit a new level that you didn't even know was there. It's the same game but so much more exciting and rewarding.

Johnny. Johnny Johnny Johnny Johnny Johnny. I asked him the other day why we got married. He said he considered me his concubine and as he approached 50, he didn't think it was right for a gentleman of his means to continue to have a concubine. He said he wanted our relationship to get better and he believed marrying would do that. He said to make me an honest woman. (See *Veracity*.)

Joke, Johnny's only. "My wife and I only argue about two things—sex and money," he says throatily, draping an arm heavily over my shoulder. "She's always upping the price."

Karate. My favorite part of karate is *kumite*

(fighting). I have begun to understand that my opponent is actually my partner and that to have fun and do well means engaging with them in a sort of dance of trust and even affection. If they have to resort to a flurry of jabs, I know I'm not paying attention. It's a long-term commitment, and you last only if you're patient. If you stay with it long enough to work things through, it gets better. And sometimes, you just gotta take your punches.

Late. Long before we were dating, we used to work out together in his basement gym. I remember sitting on the stoop of his building uptown, Johnny late for a workout appointment. I thought, "If he were my boyfriend, I'd be mad right now. But since he's not, I know it's just that he's late." I tried to remember later, when he *was* my boyfriend, not to take his habits personally, that he wasn't doing stuff to me, he was just doing it.

Liking Johnny (and a few things about him). I like his brown eyes, his jaunty 1950s walk, his curly hair, his loud laugh, the heedless way he throws himself in. His small Irish mouth, like John Cusack's. The fire down below. He's handsome, and like all poets, I am obsessed with physical beauty: the only item in our pre-nup is that if he loses his hair, he loses me. I like the way he looks at me and the way he says my name. I like that he has a flair for loving me. That he gives me all the time I need. I like the smooth skin on his back, the sounds he makes in his sleep, his dopey joke. I like that I baffle him, that I'm the love of his life, that he talks about me to the guys at work. A young artist we know, Joe Carey, made a collage of little headshots of white basketball players; look closely: there's Johnny. I married a *guy*.

Luck. How much of marital longevity comes down to luck? I felt lucky to hook up with Johnny, so I quit looking around. I felt lucky to be able to choose a husband to please myself, and not worry about money or children. Or maybe luck is just lost lunar creeley raffish cheekbone zigzag gibberish.

Money. Well, it's nice to have enough to be able to sit across from each other in a decent restaurant, holding hands.

More About Money. Standing offer: I'll pay him $100 if he ever cries.

Memory, bad. Thanks to which, neither of us can remember for long the other's sins, wrongdoings and crimes. Why was I so angry in 1999? I have no idea! I *do* remember that we decided—consciously *and* unconsciously—that we're together no matter what.

Marriage is when you can ignore him for a while when you are sick or pondering, and neither of you gets unduly apprehensive. **Marriage** is listening to him sleeping. And the anxiety that he keep breathing. **Marriage** changes everything and nothing. You're exactly the same and completely different, simultaneously.

My mother said you gotta raise 'em right, right from the start, or two years later, when they're not so in love, you won't be able to train them at all; they'll just think you're changing the rules. Lucky for me, a second wife, Johnny came broken in, and trained me without me knowing what he was up to.

Names. We're still married because he kept his name and I kept mine. He married me, he didn't adopt me! How can you be equal, fair and imposing if you're just a subset of someone else's name? No one can live your life except you, and it starts with your name.

New York Provincial. We went for a week to Montreal, which Johnny liked for two reasons:

(1) Where we stayed looked a lot like our neighborhood. I've noticed that many people like to vacation in places that are exactly like where they come from. My niece, who lives on the beach in Florida, pays extra for an ocean view room when she travels.

(2) I told him we only had to do one thing every day, and the rest of the time he could go to the gym or lie around and read. One night we went to a fancy fondue restaurant. One course was Canadian game—reindeer, caribou, musk ox—thin-sliced meat we dipped into sizzling oil. As we were leaving, I asked how he liked it. "For those prices," he said, "I don't think you should have to cook your own meal." This is a Manhattan-born man who had never eaten in a restaurant, had garlic or been to a mall till he was 40. "A New York provincial," he calls himself.

Niagara Falls. Gregory Corso's wonderful poem "Marriage" has these lines: "I kiss the bride all those corny men slapping me on the back / She's all yours, boy! Ha-ha-ha! / And in their eyes you could see some obscene honeymoon going on / Then all that absurd rice and clanky cans and shoes / Niagara Falls! Hordes of us! Husbands! Wives! Flowers! Chocolates!"

Johnny and I took separate honeymoons. I went to Europe with my friend Maggie and he went home to mother. Who went into her final decline the day after he called to tell her we'd gotten married. "Oh Johnny," she said, which come to think of it, was pretty much the only thing I ever heard her say.

My friend Alexandra lived in the same building as Corso for many years and Corso would ask her for stuff all the time, like a winter coat or a meal. One time he wanted her to find him a girlfriend. "I've got five kids with five women," he told her. "I'm good with women!"

Old Age. Once when we had broken up (which happened a lot our first few years), I saw an elderly couple in the lobby of the building where I worked. When she wrapped a scarf around his neck, that gesture of love, intimacy and long companionship made me cry. I wanted to be that couple. I wanted years of days that were much like the day before. That seemed so easy and so difficult. Of course, now that we (almost) are that couple, I realize I didn't want to be them quite so soon.

Other women. "I got rid of them, but I couldn't get rid of you."

Owners. Does "my" in "my spouse" express ownership or simply relation? New Yorkers tend not to buy houses or cars, so marriage often is our one big permanent nerve-wracking purchase. A spouse is much more exciting than a house and requires at least as much upkeep.

Perfect Marriage. I have a friend who's been married three times—for love, for a baby and for financial security. Two disasters and a shot at a third. She says she and most of her friends divorced too quickly, out of some idea that they deserved to be perfectly happy, but they basically have the same marriages over and over. As Adela Rogers St. Johns said, "There is so little difference between husbands you might as well keep the first."

Poetry. We sit in parks in the summer and read long poems out loud. Over the years we've read *Paradise Lost, Don Juan, The Prelude, Paterson* and many more. Anything that will take a whole summer.

POSSLQ, Persons of Opposite Sex Sharing Living Quarters, a 1980s census term for "unmarried partners."

Proposing. The first time Johnny proposed, we'd been seeing each other for two weeks. He asked me to take a leap of faith. "I don't think we're ready for this," I said. The next proposal came a couple years later, from me. Johnny was mad at me, in fact we had broken up, and I vaguely thought we would get back together if we got married. By the time he came around, I'd lost interest. Eight years later, we both finally wanted it at the same time. We went out to dinner and he started to get down on his knee, but another couple jostled up the aisle and the moment passed. But not the proposal.

Prove to Me (a not-very-fun game). I think it's easier to be with someone for a long time. When we were first together, I would often ask some version of "Would you stay with me if I were paralyzed from the neck down?" There wasn't a right answer, you may be sure. One day when I asked yet again, "The answer is YES," he said in a loud, definitive manner. "And now never ask me again." And I never have. That was the last-ever round of Prove to Me. Thank goodness.

Queer. The late poet Steve Carey used to say, "I'm queer for girls!"

Quotidian. At a certain point, the anecdotes and highlights run out. It's the dailiness—the quotidian—that matters. It's recognizing his tread on the steps, knowing his exact look in some specific situation. Once I called from the other room, "Can I read you something?"

He said, "Is it the caption of a *New Yorker* cartoon?"

"Oh, do I have a special voice for that?"

So it seems. His knowing this one exact thing about me seems to be as important as anything else in our whole life.

Ring. We go to a lot of theater. One time we saw Strindberg's *Dance of Death*. The couple in the play, one of those couples you pray you don't sit near on an airplane, treat each other horribly—they play malevolent pranks, call the cops on each other, lie, torment. It's clear their marriage has gone on like this for its entire 25 years. In the last scene, they're sitting in adjacent rocking chairs, holding hands. "We go on," he says. "Yes, we go on," she replies, rocking and rocking. My wedding band has "we go on" engraved on it.

Ring. Passover is the Jewish holiday of liberation. It commemorates the Exodus, the escape from slavery in Egypt. The Hebrew word for "Egypt" also means "straits," a narrow place, and every year we ponder how we are ourselves still in bondage. At a seder I attended a few years ago, we were asked to bring a symbol of personal freedom. I held up my wedding ring as a reminder that I have chosen my own life, my own relationships, my own family.

Secret. Every marriage has a secret in its core. Even if I told you ours, it would still be a secret.

Sex. We used to go to the beach at Rockaway a lot. We would drive down early, get a great parking spot, stay for a few hours and be on our way home when the incoming traffic was just getting heavy. Back in Manhattan, salty margaritas that tasted like the sea on our bodies, then home, goofy and tumbling like seals with our hot, gritty bodies.

Sex. When I worried early on that it was "just" sex between us, he said, "Good sex comes from love and understanding."

Sex. I wonder what he thinks about when we make love. One time last week I started thinking about what socks I was going to wear the next day, but usually I only think about him. I mean, I don't even really think, I think.

Systems. Along with fines (See *Fines*), we have other systems. For example, we take turns washing dishes. His week, my week, his week, my week. The week continues past Saturday night until the sink is empty. And no kibitzing on the other person's style, timing or methods. This may seem unromantic, but once they're in place, these arrangements are useful and instinctive, like traffic lights.

We also take turns with anniversaries. Whoever's year it is makes all the arrangements, and the other is (required to be) surprised and delighted. It's generally dinner and a play, but one memorable year Johnny strewed our house with rose petals.

Transition. At first your relationship is more real when you're talking it over with your girlfriends. He's an obsession but not entirely interesting in and of himself. The relationship is real when it becomes more important than your friends.

Tripping. I always knew I would be with someone who did drugs, specifically LSD. I was never interested in guys who skipped the main thing that was happening in our generation.

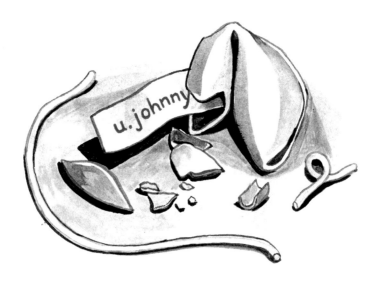

U. You. Oh, Johnny.

Veracity. Frankly, I don't see what's so great about the whole truth. I am much more of the "what they don't know won't hurt 'em" school. When God told Sarah she was going to have a baby, she laughed and said she was too old, and so was Abraham. When Abe asked God why Sarah laughed, God said, She says she's too old, omitting what she said about her husband being over the hill. The rabbis use that example of a white lie to justify shading the truth for the sake of *shalom bayit,* peace in the house.

Vehicles. In 30 years of friendship and love, Johnny and I have only ever had one "big" conversation, driving back from a family wedding in Virginia. There's an intimacy about sitting near each other in the dark that lets the confidences flow.

Wedding. I wanted to *be* married, not get married. Hence City Hall.

X, his: "nasty, brutish and short."

If we got married:

* I craved my friend's platinum ring but couldn't see shelling out $750 unless I would be wearing it for a long, long time.

* I was about to turn 40 and figured a giant and permanent crisis was better than possibly being traumatized by the new decade.

* My 10-years-younger sister was getting hitched a few months later and I thought I'd better get there first.

* I wanted to be the one who made his health decisions, if and when. And vice versa.

* I wanted to be connected to Johnny in every possible way.

* Oh yeah, sex (See *Sex*). And is anything sexier than wearing nothing but a wedding ring?

zaftig. This Yiddish word means deliciously plump and juicy, with a connotation of, well, stacked. A dish, in other words, which is probably Y Johnny married me (See *Sex*).

Acknowledgements

Thanks to Jenny Allen, Lynn Altman, Nick & Nora Charles, Lisa Gutman Schoenholt, P. Head, Avery Hurt, Martha King, Michael Lally, Glynnis Lobban, Maria Mancini, Varda Nauen, Alexandra Neil, Bob Rosenthal, Billy Sample, Abby Sosland and Steve Willis.

Elinor Nauen

Elinor Nauen grew up in Sioux Falls, South Dakota, where every kid's birthright is driving early and driving fast on roads that are "straight no potholes flat no cops." As a poet and a journalist, her work frequently focuses on cars and baseball. She is on the board of directors of The Poetry Project and, along with Martha King, hosts the Poetry Pros reading series in New York City.

She has written or edited Cars and Other Poems, American Guys, Diamonds Are a Girl's Best Friend: Women writers on baseball, Ladies, Start Your Engines: Women writers on cars and the road, and several chapbooks. So Late into the Night, a book-length poem in ottava rima, came out in Spring 2011 from Rain Mountain Press. She lives in New York City with her husband and cat.

Visit www.ElinorNauen.com for more.

Other Poetry from Cinco Puntos Press

The Resurrection of Bert Ringold
by Harvey Goldner

White Panties, Dead Friends, and Other Bits & Pieces of Love
by Bobby Byrd

Elegies in Blue
by Benjamin Alire Saenz

Incantations: *Songs, Spells and Images by Mayan Women*
by Ambar Past, Xalik Guzmán Bakbolom, and Xpetra Ernandes

For more information, visit our website at www.cincopuntos.com